THE
MONASTIC
WAY

THE

MONASTIC

WAY

M. BASIL PENNINGTON,
O.C.S.O.

CROSSROAD·NEW YORK

1990

The Crossroad Publishing Company
370 Lexington Avenue
New York, New York 10017

Printed in the United States of America
Designed by Bonni Leon

Library of Congress Cataloging-in-Publication Data

Pennington, M. Basil.
The monastic way / M. Basil Pennington.—1st ed.
p.   cm.
Bibliography: p.
ISBN 0-385-24355-3
1. Saint Joseph's Abbey (Spencer, Mass.)   2. Cistercians—
Spiritual life.   I. Title.
BX2525.S227P45   1989
271'.12'07443—dc19   89-31288
                                            CIP

CONTENTS

FOREWORD

It is with great joy and gratitude that I present this book to you. Gratitude for all that Spencer is—not just the magnificent buildings but the wonderful men who make these buildings live. I am especially grateful to Brothers Anthony, Clement, and Emmanuel for their help in gathering these photos that succeed, at least in some measure, in capturing the spirit of the Cistercian community.

Saint Joseph's Abbey, Spencer, Massachusetts, was founded in 1950 under the leadership of a great spiritual father, Dom Edmund Futterer. The community is an ancient one coming from France at the time of the French Revolution and successively finding its home in various places. A fire in the Holy Year of 1950 caused its final move from Valley Falls, Rhode Island, to Spencer. In the succeeding year the monks gathered thousands of stones and in 1952–53 put them together to create Spencer Abbey. The first Mass was celebrated in the new church on the patronal feast of the abbey, the Feast of the Assumption of the Blessed Virgin Mary, August 15, 1953. The community has grown and sent forth groups of monks to start new monasteries in other parts of the United States and South America. Today Spencer stands as one of the largest communities in the Cistercian Order, a vibrant community of monks, old and young, looking forward to the twenty-first century and its challenges, keeping an ancient heritage alive in the heart of the Church in New England.

Visitors are always welcome at the abbey. There is a small retreat-guesthouse. The church is always open for personal prayer and participation in the communal prayer of the monks. Brother Porter will welcome you.

Those who want more information about the Cistercian life may write to the Vocation Father, Saint Joseph's Abbey, Spencer, Massachusetts 01562.

May these pages bring you as much joy in beholding them as they have given us in creating them. And let me assure you of the prayers of the monks for you and yours.

—Father Basil

A

PLACE

<u>APART</u>

"Take up and read. Take up
and read." And Augustine, the
great Saint Augustine, took up
the Sacred Text and read: "Let
us live decently as people do in
the daytime: no drunken
orgies, no promiscuity or
licentiousness, and no wrangling
or jealousy. Let your armor be
the Lord Jesus Christ; forget
about satisfying your bodies
with all their cravings." It was a
moment of conversion for the
future Bishop of Hippo.

In recounting this moment in
his *Confessions*, Augustine
recalled the conversion of
Anthony, the father of
Christian monasticism, who
heard read out in the church
the text: "Go, sell all that you
have and come follow me."
Immediately the young man
took his first steps toward the
desert.

For some monks the call has been a dramatic one, a moment they will never forget. For others it has been something that quietly grew within them. For these it would be difficult to pinpoint any particular moment of call, even though the call became very deep and sure.

2

Whether a monk remembers a moment of call or not, each does quite distinctly remember the day when he went apart, the day he entered the monastic community. It was a day marked by a poignant mixture of emotions, not only for him but for all those who loved him and, in its own way, for the community that welcomed him. There was a real sense of going apart, of "leaving the world" and so many things that had for so long formed the context of life. This going apart was, of course, only a beginning; the process of untwining the heart from its acquired habits would be a long one. But the physical separation, the stepping over the threshold of the monastery, whether the road thereto be long or short, is important.

Today, perhaps, the road back to the world all too quickly becomes a short one, one that is traversed too easily and too frequently. There are so many reasons for the monk to go back down that road to the "world": visits to the doctors, blood donations, voting, meetings, institutes, seminars, visits to needy parents, and so on. As legitimate and needful as all these things are, the monk and others as well are apt to lose a sense of the importance of his going apart. The monk needs periodically to stand atop a neighboring hill, look back at the abbey, and ask himself what it means to him and to the world.

In every worthy human endeavor there is an *ideal* that calls us forth. And there is *the reality* of the here and now: our very real human weaknesses and struggles. The danger is that either we cling to the ideal, not accepting the real, and never settle, or we let go of the ideal and settle for the present "real," going nowhere—a very stagnant and disheartening way to live. The exciting challenge is to cling to the ideal, letting it ever call us forth, even as we embrace the real and bring it lovingly and gently toward the ideal.

It is important for the monk to be a man apart, and this not only physically but deeply within his spirit.

The monk's ideal is Christ: Christ, who spent most of his life in great hiddenness, who spent forty days in the desert as he prepared for his more active life, and who, during that life, again and again fled into the mountains to spend solitary nights in communion with his Father. It is for this the monk goes apart. Like his Master, he seeks the space and the time to be alone with the Father, living out and fulfilling this important aspect of Jesus' saving mission.

The monk is called to find greater freedom: freedom to live a fuller prayer life; freedom for those exercises that foster such a life: the divine office or prayer of the Church, *lectio divina* or sacred reading, silence, and humble labor; freedom to share more fully with those who live the same values and to form true community with them.

The monk is called to live this dimension of the Christ-life for all. His life apart has meaning for all the other members of the Body of Christ with whom he is intimately one. They can

7

8

rejoice not only in the fact that this dimension of the shared Christ-life is being lived and is bearing fruit for all, but also because the monk's life stands as a constant reminder that prayer and contemplation have a significant place in the life of every follower of the Master. The fact that men truly gifted by the Lord—pastors, doctors, lawyers, teachers, engineers, and so many others—are called by the Lord to forgo the exercise of their gifts and the benefits that would accrue to the Body of Christ and the human family for the sake of living this particular dimension of the Christ-life—this fact stands as a powerful witness to the importance of the contemplative dimension of the Christian life.

For this reason physical apartness is important. Not only is it a support and expression of the interior spirit of apartness so essential in a monk's life, but the whole Church needs the monk to be a man visibly apart, so that it can benefit by a clear witness to the values he seeks to live.

It is true that God said: "It is not good for man to be alone." So it is that even in his apartness the monk usually chooses a life apart but not alone.

... BUT NOT ALONE

A man who goes apart is not, of course, immediately a monk. He has embraced the monastic way of life. There will be weeks, months, and years, indeed a lifetime of growth into what a monk truly is: a Christian fully alive. Only after years of daily living of the monastic life and with the affirming discernment of his abbot and community is a man allowed to commit

himself publicly to that life
through solemn vows. Only
then is he consecrated as a
monk. One of the most
touching moments in that
ceremony comes after the actual
consecration. One by one, each
member of the community
approaches the new monk and
welcomes him into the
community with a fraternal
embrace. The love that exists
among these men is powerfully
evident.

Since the day he first entered
the monastery, the candidate
has been embraced by the
fraternal love of the brothers. In
the Cistercian community he
has found a home, a family,
and a father. Cistercian monks
follow the way of monastic life
mapped out by Benedict of
Nursia. Saint Benedict was a
very wise old spiritual father
who from decades of experience
came to know what is really at
the heart of the monastic way.
In a rather concise rule which
he wrote around 525 A.D. he
distilled this wisdom in a way
which has spoken to and guided
many thousands of monks and
nuns through the succeeding
centuries.

In the first chapter of his rule, Saint Benedict speaks of various kinds of monks. For him the cenobite, the monk who lives in community, is the *fortissimum genus,* the best kind of monk. He is the one who "wants an abbot over him," a father with a firm hand, sure in the knowledge of God and ready to teach it, experienced and ready to guide. Benedict sees the abbot aided in his teaching by many wise seniors. It is a common saying among monks that it is primarily the community that forms the newcomer. As he walks with the brethren, prays, works, studies, and converses with them, he learns what a monk is.

So the Cistercian monk prays, works, studies, and shares himself with his brothers. He knows that if he were on his own alone, he would not long persevere in rising each day at three in the morning, chanting psalms for half an hour or so, and then giving himself faithfully to a couple of hours of sacred reading and deeper prayer, prayer of the heart, contemplative prayer. But when everyone else around him is doing it, it seems quite natural. It is almost difficult not to rise and be with the others. We all know how much lighter a work load is when a loving brother is at our side working with us.

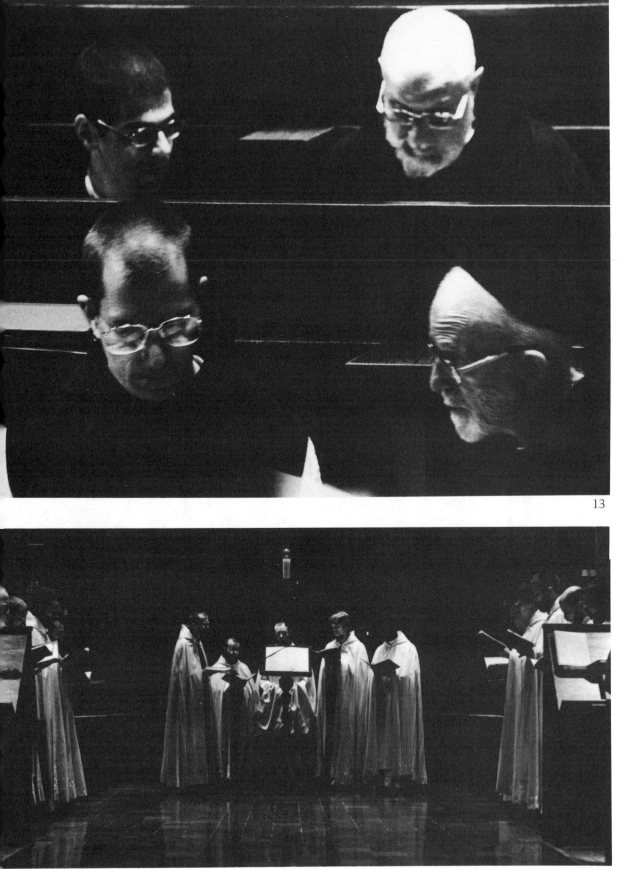

15

14

With fraternal support we go beyond ourselves, accomplishing more than we ever thought possible and finding joy in doing it.

The wisdom of the seniors, above all of the elected abbot, is there to be shared with all the brethren. The monk does not have to learn everything on his own, learn everything the hard way. As they sit together in classes or in more informal gatherings, the monks can hearten each other by sharing the graces and encouraging insights they have received on the way.

The monastic community is a family. The monks strive, as Benedict teaches, to love each other as brothers. Special care is given to those who are sick and to the older monks who are experiencing the weight of many years of loving service. Monks do, of course, find some brothers more open and friendly, others less so. They seek to learn how to love well and generously. If the Lord hadn't drawn them together, they probably would never have chosen to live with precisely all these men. Yet each one calls forth love in his own particular way and challenges his brothers to grow. Friendship is important in Christian life. It is often through a deep human friendship that we come to know what the Lord, who no longer calls us servants but friends, expects from us. The monk will find in the community a spiritual father, usually a wise old man, with whom he can confidently share all his deepest aspirations and troubles, sure of a compassionate understanding and a wise counsel. The monk will have his contemporaries with whom he shared all the joys and sorrows of the novitiate, the adventures of growing up monastically, the years of preparation for solemn vows and perhaps also ministerial priesthood. There will be brothers with whom work or common interests throw him together where a growing familiarity creates the space for deepening friendship. And there will be special friends. The Cistercian Fathers, the great spiritual writers who lived in the first days of our Order, especially Abbot Aelred of Rievaulx, have written beautiful, insightful words to guide us as we develop a deep loving friendship in Christ. The Cistercian community is a place where we learn to love—with a love that is both deeply personal

16

and truly universal, a love that finds its source in the heart of God. The Cistercian monastery is indeed "a school of love."

A
LIFE
OF
<u>WORSHIP</u>

It might be truly said that in the monastery all paths lead to the church. Whether it is individually in response to the great bell in the tower or in solemn procession with all the community, again and again the monk finds his way to the church.

Come, let us praise Yahweh
  joyfully,
acclaiming the Rock of our
  safety;
let us come into his presence with
  thanksgiving,
acclaiming him with music.
Psalm 95:1–4

Saint Benedict speaks of the monastery as a "school of the Lord's service." All the monk's life is lived in service to the Lord our God. It is, though, the divine office, the hours of prayer in choir, that the holy Legislator calls the *Opus Dei,* the work of God *par excellence.* Nothing is to be preferred to it. At times it can seem to the monks like a real "work," a labor to sing hour after hour and day after day in such a way that their minds and their hearts are fully in tune with the words of their lips. More often a monk goes to choir with a certain eagerness. Immersed in a balanced life of liturgy, *lectio divina* (sacred reading), and labor, formed and enriched more and more by the living Word of God, he longs to enter, one with his brothers, into this powerful prayer of the Church which in some way enables him to express those deeper sentiments that have grasped his spirit. He knows by experience that not only will the psalms and readings again and again open out to him moments of lightsome

insight and consolation but that they will enable him to articulate those deep sentiments of his heart that he cannot express in his own words.

Saint Benedict calls upon his monks to rise not long after the middle of the night. Cistercians usually rise around 3 A.M. to

20

come together in choir for the first office of the day, Vigils.

Forty-five minutes of psalmody and Scripture prepare him for the two hours or more that he has after the office to continue his watch for the Sun of Justice. With the dawn or soon after, the brothers gather again for an office which is simply called Praise—Lauds. Once again the Lord has given the gift of day. The rising sun reminds us how the Son of God came into our world and into our lives and how he rose from the dead. The monk lives close to the rhythms of nature, and they constantly speak to him of the God who made us.

As the day's labors begin, God
is not forgotten. Three times,
at the third, sixth, and ninth
(around 9 A.M., noon, and 3
P.M.), the monks stop their
work to pray the Hours of
Terce, Sext, and None. If they
are too far from the church,
they gather where they are
working and take a few minutes
to pray a psalm or two or three,
listen to some words from the
Scriptures, and join in the
Lord's Prayer. When the day's
labors are done, the community
celebrates the most festive of
the hours, Evening Song or
Vespers, joining the holy Virgin
Mary in magnifying God, who
has done great things for us.
The day's worship concludes
with the Hour of Compline
(around 8 P.M.) and the
heartfelt *Salve, Regina:* Hail,
Holy Queen.

At the heart and center of each
day's worship is the Eucharistic
liturgy, celebrated usually in the
morning after Lauds, before the
work of the day. On special
days it might be celebrated later
in the morning or in the
evening, in keeping with the

spirit of the particular feast. At this gathering, the Lord speaks most solemnly to the community in the proclamation of the Gospel. Here he nurtures the life of the community and of each monk with the Eucharistic bread. Here the community enters into the eternal "now" of God to be present at that most central act of all creation when the incarnate Son of God offers to the Father, on the behalf of all and in the name of all, the most perfect act of sacrificial love.

Christ remains always and ever at the center of the life of the Christian monastic community. Through him, with him, and in him the community is one and one in its being with the Father. The monk ever acknowledges Jesus as his Lord and God and worships him in the most holy Sacrament of the Altar, in his living Word, and in each person. Through the liturgical year he lives again Christ's mysteries: waiting with the prophets, celebrating his

birth with the angels and
shepherds, walking with Mary
and Joseph in his infant
mysteries, following him on the
roads of Galilee and Judea, and
living the last days of his life
with him, day by day, hour by
hour, until Christ rises from
the dead and ascends to the
Father, promising the gift of
the Holy Spirit. With the whole
Christ, the Church, monks
remain always in prayer with
Mary, the Mother of Jesus,
longing for an ever fuller
outpouring of the Spirit upon
us until all be brought to
completion in the universal
acknowledgment of the
kingship of Jesus Christ.

Day after day the monks call
upon their brother and sisters
who have gone before them
into the heavenly kingdom to
join with them in their worship.
Benedict and Bernard, Gertrude
and Mechtilde, all the monastic
saints, are close, guiding with
their example, supporting with
their prayer. In the liturgy
monks worship as a part of a
vast assembly that reaches from
their humble monastic church
up into the highest heavens.

... AND
CONTINUAL
PRAYER

A monk's worship does not end when he leaves the church and takes off his chasuble and cowl.

A statue of Benedict stands on an old stone pillar in the midst of the monastery gardens. The holy Legislator holds a finger to his lips, inviting us to abide in a continual silence. Hearts filled with worship need to pray continually.

After the communal prayer the monk may tarry in church for as long as the Spirit moves him. Or he may move out to one of the shrines or chapels about the abbey. Or step forth into the vast outdoors. Spencer Abbey stands on a hill

surrounded by hundreds of acres of open fields and wooded valleys. Roads and paths cross in all directions, inviting the monk into solitary glens or expansive vistas, each of which speaks something of the beauty of our God.

One of the monk's favorite places of prayer is the cell *(cella)*, his heaven *(caelum)* on earth. There he can precisely fulfill the Gospel mandate to go into his private room, close the door, and pray in secret to the Father.

The monk has at least three or four hours, and usually more, each day for *lectio divina*, that listening to the divine which calls forth the response of heartfelt prayer and contemplation. In this he will draw on the rich heritage of his own Cistercian tradition, but also at times on other Christian and non-Christian traditions for inspiration and guidance. After initial instruction from a novice master, he looks to a spiritual father of his own choosing for wise guidance in these ways of the Spirit.

When the monk goes into his
cell or into the quiet of the
cloister or the scriptorium, he
takes up his book and kneels
for a moment, opening himself
to the divine presence. He calls
upon the Holy Spirit who has
inspired the writer and who
dwells in him "to teach him all
things." He may listen to the
first words on his knees and
even kiss the text, reverencing
the Word in his word. He then
sits quietly and lets the Word
speak to him through the text.
There is no hurry, no need to
get on with it. The monk is not
now seeking so much to learn
new things as to be brought
into the experience of the
reality behind the words. As the
Spirit moves him, he responds.
Specific prayers may rise from
his heart. Or he may be drawn
into resting simply in the reality
revealed to him.

These quiet hours of
communion with God are at
the heart of the contemplative
life and are the reason it is
called contemplative. Here the
monk comes to know God and
all the restlessness of his restless
soul can come to rest.

Be still, and know that I am
    God.

                    Psalm 46:10

29

Although the monk might well seem to be most alone during these quiet hours in the cell, he is indeed not alone. Not only is the Lord always with him, but he is, in the Lord, intimately one with all his sisters and brothers throughout the world. As his prayer reaches for heaven, he takes all with him. Whenever any one of us rises, we all rise. The monk is leaven. The monk is a channel of divine grace and mercy. The purer he is, the more empty he is, the more the mercy of God can flow through him to this needy world of ours. The monk's time in the cell has cosmic import. The monk is for all even when he most seems to be and is for God alone. His fidelity to contemplative prayer is one of his prime responsibilities toward all his fellow mortals. Prayer is his gift and his role within the Body of the Cosmic Christ.

As the monk goes about his daily tasks his prayer accompanies him. This is why most monks have a preference for the simple, more routine sort of work; it leaves the mind freer to enter into the prayer. God is never absent from us but we want to be ever more consciously present to him with our love and thanksgiving.

With the growth of the life of the Spirit within us we become more and more conscious of God's creative presence in all that we do and in all that we use. He is in the food we eat and in the eating; he speaks to us in the reading. He is in the broom we sweep with and in the sweeping. He is in the computer and in its many amazing functions. He is never absent, always present. In our turn we seek to be lovingly present to him.

A

L I F E

OF

HUMBLE

LEARNING

The first and greatest
commandment is this:
*You shall love the Lord
your God . . . with your
whole mind . . .*
Matthew 22:37–38

Faith ever seeks a deeper, fuller understanding of the divine mysteries as they are revealed through the Sacred Scriptures, through each person, and through the whole of creation.

Saint Benedict tells the monks that they are to choose their abbot for the wisdom of his doctrine. Regularly the abbot will gather the community about him in the chapter house to share with his monks some of the wisdom he has obtained from his own studies and even more from his prayer and his experience of life.

Someone asked Abbot Anthony, "What must I do in order to please God?" The elder replied, "Pay attention to what I tell you: whoever you may be, always have God before your eyes; whatever you do, do it according to the testimony of the Scriptures; in whatever place you live, do not easily leave it. Keep these three precepts and you will be saved."

Abbot Pambo asked Abbot Anthony, "What ought I to do?" and the elder said to him, "Do not trust in your own righteousness, do not worry about the past, but control your tongue and your stomach."

32

33

A man asked Abbot Benjamin, "Give me a word." The elder said, "If you observe the following, you can be saved: Be joyful at all times, pray without ceasing, and give thanks for all things."

All the days of his life the cenobitic monk can expect to be nourished in this way. He will be encouraged to enter ever more deeply into the mysteries of God, walk more closely with Christ, and discover more fully the healing and wholing way of the monastic life as set forth by Saint Benedict.

36

The newcomer to the
monastery is entrusted to a
novice master, a man chosen
for his wisdom and prudence.
This spiritual father will seek
with the help of others to
impart to the novice the
richness of the Cistercian
heritage, the ways of the Lord
in the monastic life and how to
respond to them. When the
young man has completed this
basic formation, he will join the
other young religious for a
series of courses aimed at
grounding a lifetime of personal
study of Sacred Scripture, the
monastic Fathers and Mothers,
patristics, and the teaching of
the contemporary Church.

After his consecration as a monk, an event which usually takes place only at the end of six or seven years of preparation, if the young man senses a call to serve the community in the ministerial priesthood and this call is confirmed by the abbot and community, he will pursue the formal course of studies required for ordination. For all the monks the possibility of further studies is open according to their own attraction and needs and the needs of the community.

Courses, seminars, and special lectures are regularly offered to the whole community along with videotape presentations of current interest.

38

Although he has gone apart, the monk remains a concerned and caring member of the human family and keeps himself informed in regard to the important events of our times. He prepares himself to vote intelligently. And sometimes he might even raise his voice or pen in response to some pressing need for social justice. One of the most heard social critics in the latter part of this century in America has been a Cistercian monk: Thomas Merton. While he used his skills and powerful pen to help all realize that contemplation is not the privilege of a chosen few but the necessary fulfillment of every human life, at the same time he raised consciousness in regard to the moral implications of war and peace, economic oppression, and racial discrimination. He knew from the depths of his contemplation, as does every monk, that concern for social justice is an integral part of living the Gospels as a disciple of Jesus Christ.

However rich might be the teaching of the abbot or varied the classes and seminars, the sacred reading and study, the teacher *par excellence* is the Holy Spirit of God. "The Spirit, the Advocate, will teach you all things, calling to mind all that I have spoken to you," says the Lord. "Eye has not seen, nor ear heard, nor has it

entered into the human mind what God has prepared for those who love him, but the Spirit makes it known to us." Year after year, the monk, with the help of the Liturgy and the Fathers as well as the best of today's scholars, searches the Scriptures, listening to the Holy Spirit, who leads us ever more deeply into the reality of our oneness in and with Christ.

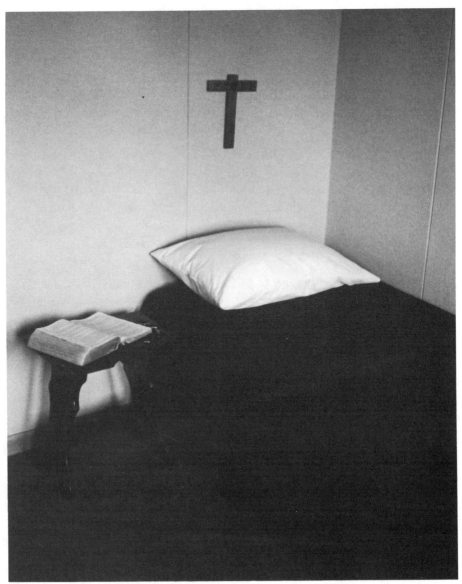

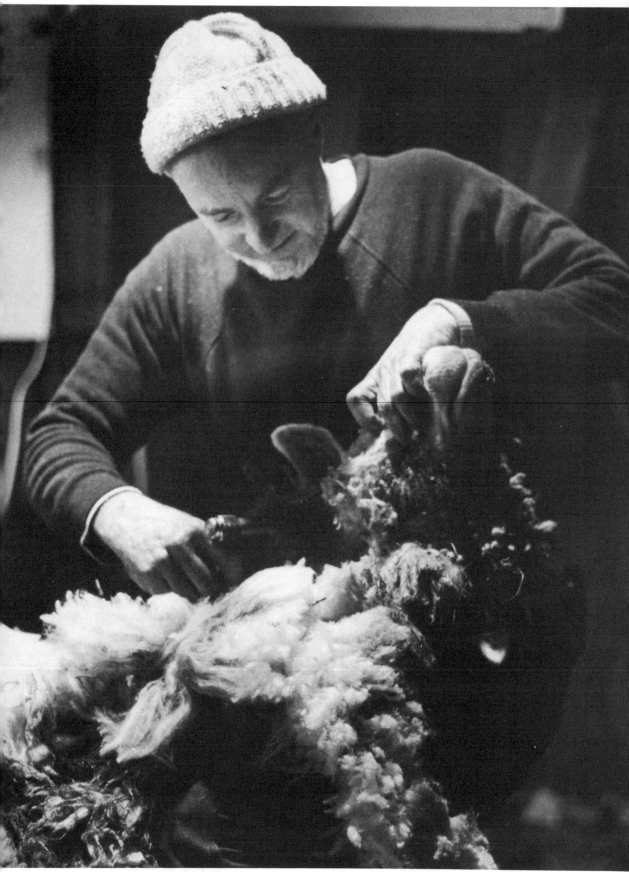

... AND OF HUMBLE LABOR

Then are they truly monks when they live by the labor of their own hands.

Saint Benedict

The first penance imposed on sinful man by his betrayed Creator was that of redeeming and fruitful work: "By the sweat of your brow you shall earn your bread." Monks do not exempt themselves from this. Each monastery seeks not only to earn its living but also to earn some surplus to share with less fortunate sisters and brothers.

Agriculture has traditionally been the favored work. Saint Basil recommended it as the best work for monks, giving many reasons for this. It most immediately addresses the needs of the monks and those of their neighbors and keeps the monks close to the rhythms of nature, dependent on their Creator, who sends the rain and the snow, clear skies and the ripening sun. Their humanity is enriched by caring association with cows and sheep and other mortals.

Today, with the domination of agribusiness and government subsidies, few monasteries can hope to support themselves on agriculture alone, though most still maintain at least a modest farm program, raising some fruits and vegetables and keeping a few animals. But this is supplemented or largely displaced by some form of industry.

41

It has not always been easy for a community to decide into which industry they should direct their efforts. Some have tried one after another before they came upon one that can adequately support the community without overburdening the brethren or requiring too much commercial involvement. Prayer and communal discernment allows the monks to be guided by Divine Providence to the

enterprise that will best suit the community and the local conditions. In order to be recognized as an autonomous abbey a monastic community must establish that it can support itself by its own labor.

46

At Spencer Abbey the monks have developed Trappist Preserves, producing some of the finest jams and jellies on the market. Factory work does not blend as well into the balance of the traditional monastic life, or so it seems to some. Machines have their own rhythm, as do the secular markets, and the monks have to conform to these if they are to succeed in their modest enterprises. The physical exercise that the monk used to find in field and garden now often has to be made up in jogging or walking or other exercises or in an occasional game of volley ball. But the daily toil in the factory to the tune of high-tech automation enables the monk to realize a certain solidarity with many of his sisters and brothers and gives witness that such labor does not preclude the quest for holiness or a life intimately united with Christ the laborer from Nazareth.

49

Still, more creative work will probably always be some monks' preference. Through the Holy Rood Guild the monks of Spencer have found a way to offer scope to many creative hands and eyes in an undertaking that not only contributes to the support of the community but enhances the liturgical life of the Church with fine vestments and beautiful liturgical vessels. After the sheep are shorn, there is weaving and dyeing. Colors are to be blended and designs drawn: chasubles, copes, and stoles; then cutting and sewing in the tradition of fine tailoring. Chalices and communion vessels are molded and baked, or shaped in copper and enameled. Incense and chrism are blended with care. A multitude of gifts is employed. And still the business of sales and inventory and accounting remains to be done.

As with any community, besides the labor that earns our daily bread there are many other tasks that keep the monastery going and make it a beautiful home: maintenance of all sorts, cooking and baking, washing and cleaning, care for the sick, and a welcome for the guests. The monks' work is never done, yet the sharing makes the labor light: from each according to his ability and gifts. Most monks work only about five hours a day at community tasks and income-earning labors, though monasteries are usually blessed with some brothers who are called to seek God and serve him and their brothers in longer hours of prayerful work, giving perhaps less time to the choral office and sacred reading. Each monk works out his personal rhythm with his spiritual father and the blessing of the abbot, taking into account the needs of his brothers.

With a joyful heart we seek to embrace our daily cross of labor in union with Jesus of Nazareth, the carpenter, who earned his daily bread by the sweat of his brow and so inspired his apostles.

A RETURN TO SIMPLICITY

The potter throws his clay on the turning wheel. He feels good as he wets his hands and begins to mold the lump. He feels the clay's texture, its every little flaw, its potential to be the pot that as yet exists only deep within him. Eye and hand and foot, his whole body must be one with his intention, undistracted if the image is to become a reality.

52

The divine Potter is at work. He gives us the dignity and glory—and the responsibility to be one with him as he molds a vessel for the most noble of purposes: to be the chosen dwelling place of the Divine forever. It is because he wants to be an undistracted participant in this all-important task that the monk chooses to go apart and seek a life and an environment that will reflect and support his singleness of purpose.

The monk chooses a life that is gently but firmly ordered by a rule so that he can expect day to follow upon day with the steady, simple, yet awesome rhythm of a monastic cloister. His home, its garden enclosed, its cloister walks, its church of austere beauty, its modest cells—all seek to leave his life uncluttered, free, supported in its singleness of direction— designed to leave all the doors to the Divine wide open so that the deifying light may enter unhindered. The furnishings are sparse and spare, what will support life and not encumber it. The clothing is what is needed.

The cowl of the Cistercian is an ample white garment—no pleats or appendages. An ample embrace enfolding the monk in contemplation.

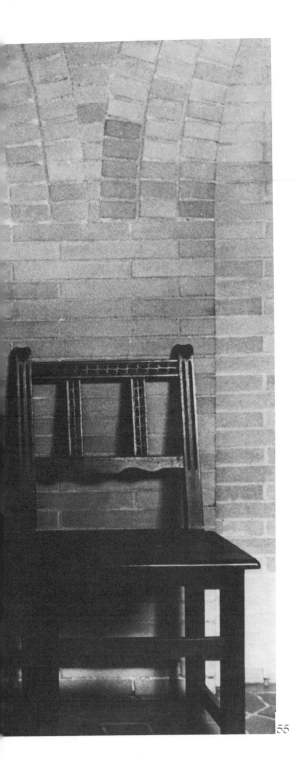

The Master has said, "Unless you become as a little one, you cannot enter the kingdom." The monk in many ways opts to be a little one, living always in his Father's house, expecting all things from the father of the monastery, doing what he is told, free to devote his attention to the one thing necessary. With as pure a heart as possible, he seeks the kingdom of God and his justice, confident that his heavenly Father will take care of everything.

Nowhere is this mature, childlike simplicity as transparently evident as in the faces of the seniors. There comes to my mind's eye now a whole procession of such faces: Brother Francis, the Polish wrestler who worked his way across Russia and down into the States. In his last years he wrestled with cancer. The walk up the hill from his shoe shop to the abbey became a veritable climb for him, yet his labored steps were always accompanied by a jingling rosary and a broad smile. Brother Alfred, who came in his forties, was another who always had his rosary in hand and a smile on his face. He quietly used his Wall Street skills to help build the abbey. Father Raymond came to the cloister after thirty-five years in the diocesan priesthood. After many more fruitful years in the abbey guesthouse, when his legs could carry him no farther than the infirmary chapel, he was content to sit there before the Lord all the day long, praying

57

58

for all those to whom he had ministered. Brother Vincent had spent most of his sixty-five years in the monastery at the porter's lodge, welcoming each of us. When we gathered to anoint him, he promised to be at the gate of heaven to see us safely in. One thing all our seniors surely have in common is this: as the years roll on, their smiles become more and more constant, more gentle—if I may say it, more sweet, more pervasive, more heartwarming. Oftentimes the joy of heaven seems to be already invading them, even in the midst of prolonged and painful illnesses. There is something truly childlike in the way they receive life and accept all that comes along.

"Unless you become as a little one, you cannot enter the kingdom."

... BY AN ORDINARY

W A Y

Yes, monks eat and eat
heartily—usually three times a
day. We gather only at noon
for a formal meal, when one of
the brothers feeds our minds
and hearts with reading while
we feed our bodies, but most
monks find their way to the
refectory in the early hours of
the day for a cup of coffee and
some cereal or hearty slices of
homemade bread. And again in
the evening for some soup or
salad, a sandwich or pasta.

If monks eat, it means there are
dishes to do. And you can
guess who does them! It also
means that Father Aidan and
Brother Patrick spend long
hours in the kitchen creating
tasty meals of vegetables and

pasta, eggs, and an occasional
fish. And fresh salads, too, and
desserts with calories beyond
counting.

---

*Whether you eat or drink or
whatever else you do, do all for
the glory of God.*
                    1 Corinthians 10:31

60

Monks seek to go to God by a very simple and direct way but always by a human way. If he does "love fasting," he also loves feasting. He knows that cleanliness, if not next to godliness, is not foreign to it. There are not only dishes to be washed, but clothes, and windows, and floors, and many other things. There is dusting and mopping and vacuuming and all the other household tasks. They are all part of our way to God.

There is indoor work and there is outdoor work. There are lawns to be mowed, hedges to be trimmed, gardens to be tended, and woodlots to be thinned. And how many other labors. And they are all part of our way to God.

Technology is not foreign to the day and way of the monk. Computers save him hours for *lectio* and prayer. And help him write new *lectio* if that be his task. Copiers have replaced the copyists. Mixers and cookers, bottlers and cappers, pasteurizers and labelers enable twelve monks to turn out tons of perserves in a morning so they can be free in the afternoon for study and prayer, for long walks and long meetings, for exercise and fellowship.

64

63

Hobbies, too, are part of the monastic day and way.

Music has its favored place, both the listening and the playing. Our New Year's celebration brings together a wondrous collection of instruments: piano, organ, clarinet, trombone, bass electric guitar (as well as several other types), recorders, drums, violin, and mandolin; even an accordion and a harmonica have been known to show up. The visual arts are well represented also: oils, crayon, pencil, charcoal, ceramics, enamels, wood carving and metalworking, weaving and needlework, calligraphy and illumination. Of course, there is gardening too. It is a joy to share the fruits of all of these in community.

Monks are human. And nothing human is foreign to them. But they are careful about what they do integrate into their way and their day. For they seek to integrate all into a simple, direct response to God in whose divine simplicity all things find their ultimate being and meaning.

65

67

*Who will give me wings like a
dove, to fly away and find rest?*

Psalm 55:6

GREATER SOLITUDE

There is something very deep in every human spirit that seeks at times a deeper quiet and solitude—to be alone with oneself and find one's true self deep in God. To go beyond the ordinary boundaries that seem to fence us in. To penetrate more deeply the mystery of life—our own mystery: who am I, this person made in the very image of God; who is this God, who so penetrates me, who so loves me, who gives me the gifts of life and love and hope?

Especially when the earth is cloaked in the silence of night or cowled in Cistercian white by winter's snow and all is hushed—then these deeper longings emerge and draw us within. When the vast white expanse reaches out before us to meet the unlimited horizon. . . . We are called.

The monk is the privileged one who has received the grace and the gift to respond to that call, not in a momentary way or for a time of quickly passing retreat but with resolute steps and permanent commitment. We go apart to be in solitude to attend ever more fully to things divine.

The Cistercian life offers a unique blend of the values of solitude and the loving support of a community of sisters or brothers. In the monastery all is geared to allow each to be free to be with God and to support each in a faithful response to his or her call.

Deep in the heart of every true monk there is a yearning for ever greater solitude.

Tucked away in the woods and hollows of the monastic domain there are a number of little hermitages where each monk may, from time to time, take a day or a week to be alone with God. It can be a time of most blessed encounter. Or it can be a time of renewed struggle with the false self and all its imperious demands. Solitude is a place where pretense cannot long survive. Lines are drawn; real choices are made.

69

Some few monks experience the call to greater solitude more persistently. With the blessing of their abbot and community, they may be permitted to enter into the eremitical life more permanently. This will usually be in some suitable corner of the monastic domain where the hermit will still be protected by the overreaching mantle of the abbey. In some instances a Cistercian might be called to settle in some more distant solitude, returning to his community only on rare occasions. Absent in body, Cistercian hermits always remain very much in the community. Their example of courageous fidelity inspires and encourages their brethren just as the Church as a whole is inspired and encouraged by its contemplative communities.

Each of us ultimately will be called to the great solitude. We will have to leave all behind and pass into the unknown alone. It has meaning beyond words to have at the hour of passing the

brethren gathered around, the
quiet chant of their prayer
embracing and supporting.
Each goes ahead alone but not
unaccompanied. A lifetime of
love enfolds.

The monk knows in the truest sense he will never leave the community. Loving prayer will surround him as the community celebrates his passing from life to life—the life that does not end. Funerals are among the greatest celebrations in a monastery. The monk's body is laid to rest in the midst of the brethren. A white cross stands over him, proclaiming his victory in Christ, assuring all the brethren that he will be there together with them when all rise with Christ.

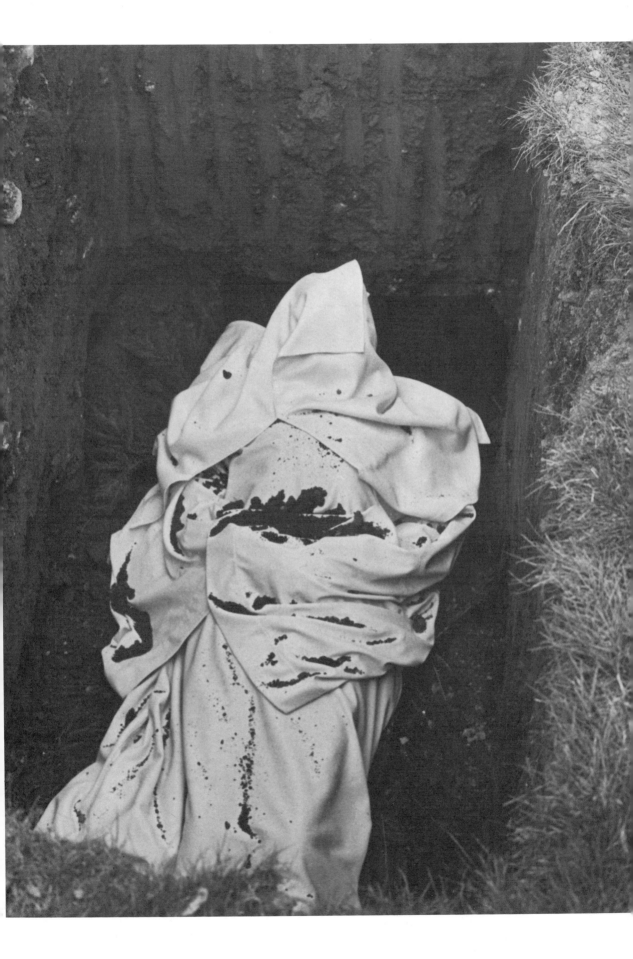

74

73

Each day the brethren, as they pass down the cloisters, still on the journey of life, pause to commune with those who have gone before. They know that the departed are very much alive in the Lord, that they will by God's grace someday lie beside them, that they will all rise together.

We are alone in death, but never less alone. Truly *monos*, alone, yet one. All the barriers fall away. Our absolute oneness in Christ—even as he is one with the Father—is achieved. In the end there will be but one Christ, loving himself—all will be one in him in perfect love.

GUESTS

ARE

WELCOME

A monk's love, therefore, does
not stop with his monastic
family. The lamp is always
shining by the front door of the
monastery. There is always a
Brother Porter or a Father
Guestmaster ready to speak a
word of welcome. Christ comes
to us not only in relatives and
friends but also in strangers,
and above all in the poor and
needy.

The person who enters the monastery is a loving person; otherwise he would never think of entering "the school of love." He has come from a family he loves deeply. The separation is usually difficult, more so for his family. The monk gains a whole new family, a father and many brothers. His family loses a son—not really, of course, but it seems that way. So a very special care and concern is shown by the monks toward the families of their brethren. They want them to realize that they, too, have gained a new family, that the monastery is their son's home where they are most welcome.

The fact is that everyone belongs to the monk's family, the family of God. Each one who comes is welcomed as a brother or sister, as Christ himself. The monastery grounds are always open. One can walk by the lake or along the roads and quietly commune with nature. Or enter the church and pray before the Blessed Sacrament. There are always monks available for a quiet visit or a word of counsel. Unfortunately limitation of

75

space makes it necessary to call in advance if one wants to spend the night, but over a thousand do each year. Many come for a weekend or a five-day retreat, entering into the life of prayer of the monks and enjoying quiet hours for solitary reflection and prayer.

The monastery is never without guests. The monks' lives are enriched by the sharing of their guests—their stories touch us and keep us in touch with the everyday life of the Church, their courage in following Christ edifies and encourages us, their needs call us forth and goad us on to more fervent and sustained prayer. And we hope that they go away with a deeper peace, a clearer realization of how much they are loved by God.

Some groups return to us regularly year after year, like the men from the Brooklyn Navy Yard or the Fire Fighters of New York. I have been very touched as I have listened to them speak of what their time at the abbey means to them: "Eight years ago, I was involved in the Hotel Vendome in which nine of my brothers died. I took a ride down five floors and I was buried for twenty-five minutes, and in twenty-five minutes you have quite a long time to talk with God. During that time he and I came to a solid understanding. And this is what I come up here for, to renew that understanding. We see monks in prayer here, the solitude and the quiet and . . . I want to get a little piece of that feeling.

You know, we're out there in the wild world, sort of, and that aura that they have about them, I want a little to rub off on me."

Retreatants while with us make their home in the small retreat-guesthouse attached to the abbey. Like the abbey itself, this house has its cloister, chapel, refectory, and meeting rooms. The retreatants join the monks for the liturgical services in the abbey church: Vigils at 3:30 A.M. (if they wish), Lauds and Mass at 6:40, Vespers at 5:40 P.M. and Compline at 7:40. There is reading during the meals in the retreat house so that the spirit is nourished along with the body. And on most days there is a conference given by one of the monks who is also available for private consultation. Much time is left for the retreatant to enjoy the silence and solitude. Some of the guestrooms even have their own private garden. The men are free to join in conversation with one another and with the guestmaster and to enjoy walks together along the road to the lake and the Porter's Lodge. Some of the monks have been ordained priests, and these men are available to the retreatants for the celebration of the sacrament of reconciliation.

While a monastery must always remain a place apart if it is going to be true to itself and its particular role within the Body of Christ, it is not on the outer fringes of the Church but rather deep within its heart. Men come to the monastic life to seek purity of heart within the heart of Christ. And they welcome into their solitude men who are true seekers and want to come apart for a time to engage more intimately in this quest. They welcome all to join with them in entering into that prayer of praise which rises incessantly from the heart of the Church.

Guests are welcome!

IN HONOR OF THE BLESSED VIRGIN MARY

Salve, Regina . . .

Hail, holy Queen!

What can we say about Mary?

The title of Queen is foreign to
us and makes her foreign to us.
Yet she is, indeed, the Queen
of All Hearts.

Above all and before all, she is
mother. Mother of the Savior,
she brings him to the world and
to each one of us. She is our
mother—our life, our
sweetness, our hope.

There is no doubt to whom the
abbey belongs. As we approach
it, there in the center of the
front porch she waits with her
Son—a gentle mother assuring
a gentle welcome.

When we come into the
church, we behold her
enthroned in majesty, crowned
with stars, the moon beneath
her feet, the Child who rules
with rod of iron standing on
her knees. Joep Nichol's
magnificent "Salve" window
dominates the whole church, a

vibrant presence which becomes
more vibrant as the rising sun
brings it to life. Each evening,
when the day has come to its
fullness, the weary monks find
a new energy, sparked by love,
as the great window is
illuminated, candles are lit, and
all come to attention, "standing
in ceremony," to chant the
ancient hymn:

Salve, Regina,
  Mater misericordiae,
vita, dulcedo, et spes nostra,
  salve.
Ad te clamamus,
  exsules filii Evae,
ad te suspiramus,
  gementes et flentes,
in hac lacrimarum valle.
Eia ergo, Advocata nostra,
illos tuos misericordes oculos
  ad nos converte.
Et Jesum,
  benedictum fructum ventris tui
nobis post hoc exsilium ostende,
O clemens, O pia, O dulcis
  Virgo Maria

Hail, Holy Queen,
  Mother of mercy,
our life, our sweetness,
  and our hope.
To you do we cry, poor
  banished children of Eve,

to you do we send up our sighs,
  mourning and weeping
  in this valley of tears.
Turn then, most gracious
  Advocate,
your eyes of mercy toward us.
And after this our exile
  show unto us
the blessed Fruit of your womb,
  Jesus,
O clement, O loving, O sweet
  Virgin Mary.

Legend has it that it was in the
great cathedral of Spire. The
canons were completing their
beautiful salute to Mary, which
was written in the ninth
century by Herman the Little,
when Saint Bernard, lost in
ecstasy, added the final words:
*O clemens, O pia, O dulcis
Virgo Maria.*

Mary's presence is pervasive in
the monastery just as it is
pervasive in the lives of her
monks. In the cloister, in the
library, in the various chapels,
in the monks' cells, in the
gardens, and in the cemetery
she is to be found—found in
her many guises: queen,
mother, maiden, lady—always a
gentle, loving presence bringing
sweetness and gentleness to
strong male lives.

82

Mary has her unique theological role. She is the one through whom God came to us, entering our human race. Through her, redemption and salvation came to us and continue to come to us in her constant mediation and loving care.

Every Cistercian abbey is dedicated to Mary. The full title of Saint Joseph's Abbey is actually the Abbey of Blessed Mary of Saint Joseph—the name Mary was known by when she walked the streets of Nazareth and fulfilled her motherly tasks in the home: Mary of Joseph. It is in this more familial and intimate guise that most of us experience Mary today. She is present in our midst as a caring mother. Her presence, as a mother's, is pervasive in the home, perhaps taken in large part for granted, but so essential to the good order and peace of the household. Always there, it is in our sorrows perhaps even more than in our special joys that we turn to her and find so much consolation and strength.

Our medieval forebears saw her more as "Our Lady"—mother of their Lord. They were her serfs. Though this imagery is foreign to us today, we no less sense our belonging to her. Some monks bear her name, received when they became monks of the abbey; all monks are her sons.

And her disciples. We have much to learn from Mary, the most perfect disciple. Her "Yes" to the Lord is the model for monks. Its fruitfulness bespeaks the fruitfulness their lives can have, both for themselves and for our world if they but live their own "Yes" to God. Mary's song, her *Magnificat*, is the model for monastic worship: truly humble, truly exultant, filled with concern for all, a cry for social justice. Mary turns the water of life, all salty tears, unto the wine of celebration and joy. And pointing to her Son, she gives us the best advice: "Do whatever he tells you." She is, indeed, mother, mothering the divine life in her monks.

Hail, Holy Queen, Mother . . .

SELECT BIBLIOGRAPHY

Cistercian Fathers Series and Cistercian Studies Series, ed. E. Rozanne Elder et al. (Kalamazoo, Mich.: Cistercian Publications, 1969–).

Batselier, Peter, *Saint Benedict: Father of Western Civilization* (Antwerp: Mercatorfonds, 1980).

Benedict of Nursia, *RB 1980* (Collegeville, Minn.: The Liturgical Press, 1980).

Dechanet, Jean-Marie, O.S.B., *William of Saint Thierry: The Man and His Works* (Spencer, Mass.: Cistercian Publications, 1972).

Fracchia, Charles, *Living Together Alone* (San Francisco, Calif.: Harper & Row, 1978).

Gallois, Genevieve, O.S.B., *The Life of Little Saint Placid* (New York: Pantheon, 1956).

Gregory the Great, *The Life and Miracles of Saint Benedict*, trans. by Alexius Hoffman, O.S.B. (Collegeville, Minn.: The Liturgical Press, 1925).

Hart, Patrick, O.C.S.O., ed., *The Monastic Journey* (Mission, Kans.: Sheed, Ward and McNeil, 1977).

———, *Thomas Merton, Monk: A Monastic Tribute* (Mission, Kans.: Sheed, Ward and McNeil, 1977).

Knowles, David, O.S.B., *Christian Monasticism* (New York: McGraw-Hill, 1961).

Leclercq, Jean, O.S.B., *Bernard of Clairvaux and the Cistercian Spirit* (Kalamazoo, Mich.: Cistercian Publications, 1976).

———, *The Love of Learning and the Desire for God: A Study of Monastic Culture* (New York: Fordham University Press, 1961).

Lekai, Louis, O. Cist., *The Cistercians, Ideals and Reality* (Kent, Ohio: Kent State University Press, 1985).

Merton, Thomas, O.C.S.O., *The Sign of Jonas* (New York: Harcourt, Brace, 1953).

———, *The Waters of Siloe* (New York: Harcourt, Brace, 1949).

Nouwen, Henri, *The Genesee Diary* (Garden City, N.Y.: Doubleday, 1976).

Pennington, M. Basil, O.C.S.O., *Jubilee: A Monk's Journal* (New York: Paulist Press, 1981).

———, *Monastery* (San Francisco: Harper & Row, 1983).

———, ed., *The Cistercian Spirit* (Spencer, Mass.: Cistercian Publications, 1969).

———, *Contemplative Community* (Spencer, Mass.: Cistercian Publications, 1972).

———, *One Yet Two: Monastic Tradition East and West* (Kalamazoo, Mich.: Cistercian Publications, 1976).

———, *Rule and Life* (Spencer, Mass.: Cistercian Publications, 1971).

Squire, Aelred, O.P., *Aelred of Rievaulx* (Kalamazoo, Mich.: Cistercian Publications, 1981).

LIST OF ILLUSTRATIONS

Code:
A = Archives of Saint Joseph's Abbey;
BP = Father Basil Pennington, O.C.S.O.;
CF = Brother Clement Fornier, O.C.S.O.;
EM = Brother Emmanuel Morenelli, O.C.S.O.;
MN = Mark Nelson;
PQ = Brother Paul Quenen, O.C.S.O.;
+ = death years.

26. EM
27. Brother Thomas (+ 1988). BP
28. Library. A
29. Brother Moses. EM
30. PQ
31. Brother Jude in the solarium. BP
32. Abbot Augustine giving a talk in the chapter house. EM
33. Father Bernard leading a class in the novitiate. EM
34. Father Basil conducting a class with the young professed monks. MN
35. Father Owen, senior of the community, studying in the scriptorium. EM
36. Brother Robert in the library. BP
37. Library. EM
38. Brother Simon in the library. EM
39. Brother Gerard in his cell. EM
40. The cell of a monk. EM
41. BP
42. Father Robert shearing the sheep. CF
43. Brother David in the vegetable garden. BP
44. Father Adrian mixing the preserves. CF
45. Brother Simon cutting cloth to make a sacerdotal vestment. EM
46. Father Joseph. EM
47. Brother Gabriel. BP
48. Brother Terence. EM
49. Brother Gerard. CF
50. Brother Gerard. CF
51. The potter. BP
52. An ancient clay pot. EM
53. The east cloisters. MN
54. The door leading to the abbot's tower. MN
55. Mailboxes. PQ
56. EM
57. CF
58. Brother Thomas (+ 1988) EM
59. Community refectory. EM
60. Community kitchen. BP
61. Brother Benedict in the refectory. EM
62. Brother Simon in the library. EM
63. Brothers Anthony and David. EM
64. Brother Gregory. EM
65. Brother Mark Allen. EM
66. EM
67. MN
68. BP
69. One of the hermitages. BP
70. The funeral of Brother Thomas. EM
71. The funeral of Brother Thomas. EM
72. The burial. EM
73. Cloisters leading to the refectory. EM

74. EM
75. Wrought-iron lamp by the door of the cottage. MN
76. Brother Matthew Joseph in the Porter's Lodge. CF
77. Father Damian, the guestmaster, welcoming a guest at the front door of the guesthouse. BP
78. Brother Ephrem with his family on the day of his solemn profession. CF
79. In the guesthouse parlor. EM
80. Sculpture on the porch of the abbey church. CF
81. Window over the main altar in the abbey church, east wall. A
82. Byzantine Chapel. EM
83. Garden Shrine. BP
84. Guesthouse Shrine. EM
85. Our Lady of Lourdes, a statue that stood in the façade of the church of the Abbey of Our Lady of the Valley, now in the gardens at Spencer Abbey. Henry J. Hoffman.

CISTERCIAN
MONASTERIES
IN THE
UNITED
STATES
AND
CANADA

(An asterisk after the name of the monastery indicates that it belongs to the "Cistercian Order"; otherwise it is of the "Cistercian Order of the Strict Observance," often called "Trappists.")

Houses of Monks
New Clairvaux Abbey
P.O. Box 37
Vina, CA 96092

Saint Benedict's Abbey
1012 Monastery Road
Snowmass, CO 81654

Holy Spirit Monastery
2625 Highway 212 S.W.
Conyers, GA 30208-4044

New Melleray Abbey
Dubuque, IA 52001

Gethsemani Abbey
Trappist, KY 40051

St. Joseph's Abbey
Spencer, MA 01562

Assumption Abbey
Route 5, Box 193
Ava, MO 65608

Cistercian Monastery*
Hainesport—Mt. Laurel Road
Mount Laurel, NJ 08054

Genesee Abbey
Piffard, NY 14533

Guadalupe Abbey
Box 97
Lafayette, OR 97127

Monastery of Saint Mary*
R.D. 1, Box 206
New Ringgold, PA 17960

Mepkin Abbey
HC 69, Box 800
Moncks Corner, SC 29461-9722

Abbey of Our Lady of Dallas*
1 Cistercian Road
Irving, TX 75039

Holy Trinity Abbey
1250 S. 9500 E.
Huntsville, UT 84317

Holy Cross Abbey
Route 2, Box 3870
Berryville, VA 22611

Spring Bank Abbey*
Rt. 3, Box 159
Sparta, WI 54656

Monastère de N.–D. du Calvaire
R.R. 3, Boîte 25
Rogersville, N.B., E0A 2T0
CANADA

Abbaye N.-D. des Prairies
C.P. 310
Holland, Man R0G 0X0
CANADA

Abbaye Cistercienne
100, route des Trappistes
Mistassini, P.Q., G0W 2C0
CANADA

Abbaye Notre-Dame du Lac
1600, Chemin d'Oka, R.R. 1
Oka, P.Q., J0N 1E0
CANADA

Abbaye de N.-D. de Nazareth*
C.P. 99
Rougemont, P.Q., J0L 1M0
CANADA

Houses of Nuns
Santa Rita Abbey
HCR 929
Sonoita, AZ 85637

Redwoods Monastery
Whitethorn, CA 95489

Mississippi Abbey
8400 Abbey Hill Road
Dubuque, IA 52001

Mount St. Mary's Abbey
300 Arnold Street
Wrentham, MA 02093

Our Lady of the Angels Monastery
Route 2, Box 288-A
Crozet, VA 22932

Monastery of the Valley of Our Lady*
E 11096 Yankee Drive
Prairie du Sac, WI 53578-9737

Abbaye de l'Assomption d'Acadie
Rogersville, N.B. E0A 2T0
CANADA

Abbaye Cistercienne
Saint-Romuald
C.P. 3999 Terminus
Lévis, P.Q. G6V 6V4
CANADA

ABOUT THE AUTHOR

Father M. Basil Pennington, O.C.S.O., is a Trappist monk and priest at St. Joseph's Abbey in Spencer, Massachusetts. He entered the Cistercian Order in 1951 after graduating from Cathedral College, Brooklyn, NY. After ordination in 1956, he spent several years studying in Rome. He assisted at the Second Vatican Council as a peritus and in the preparation of the new Code of Canon Law. With Thomas Merton, he started Cistercian Publications in 1968 and founded the Institute of Cistercian Studies at Western Michigan University in 1973. Father became nationally known through his efforts to help the American Church refind its contemplative dimension through the Centering Prayer Movement. For four years, he served as a vocational father in his Order, lecturing widely and publishing a book on vocational discernment. Father has published over twenty books and some four hundred articles in various languages. His most recent publications are *Mary Today*, published at the opening of the Marian Year, a personal study of Thomas Merton, *Thomas Merton—Brother Monk*, and a book of spirituality for priests.